AF413253

The Cost of Freedom

From Despair to Liberty: A Perilous Escape

By

Hien Dang

Dedication

This book is lovingly dedicated to my late parents. Their unwavering support and sacrifices allowed my brother and me to escape despite the immense emotional, financial, and life-threatening risks.

I dedicate this book to my two children, whose inspiration drove me to write it. I hope that they will comprehend the challenging and dangerous journey I undertook to attain freedom.

Acknowledgments

I extend my sincere gratitude to my brother for assisting me in our escape and providing unwavering support throughout the entire journey. Without his assistance, I might not have attained the freedom I now enjoy.

I would like to extend my sincere appreciation to my wife for her steadfast support and encouragement throughout the process of writing this book. Her invaluable feedback from the initial drafts to the final manuscript and her design of the front and back cover pages have been instrumental in the completion of this work.

About the Author

Hien Dang was born in Tay Ninh, South Vietnam, and came to the U.S. as a refugee in 1981. He earned his Bachelor of Science in Electrical Engineering at North Carolina State University and relocated to Southern California, where he worked for defense companies for over three decades.

This is his first book. He is retired and lives in Southern California with his wife and two young adult children.

Preface

The narrative is authored by Hien Dang, detailing his journey of leaving the country by land and subsequent resettlement. As a legal entity in third countries, he holds the status of a political refugee.

This year, 2025, marks 50 years since North Vietnam took control of South Vietnam and, for me personally, 45 years since I left my homeland.

Although half a century has elapsed, it feels as if it happened only recently. Time indeed passes swiftly. I endured five years living under the strict regime of Communism. Reflecting on history confirms an undeniable reality concerning Vietnam: millions of Vietnamese citizens were forced to leave the country, with innumerable individuals losing their lives either at sea or within deep forests. There was a common saying from that period among people in South Vietnam: "If the light pole could walk, sooner or later, it would escape."

Like millions of others, I sought freedom through escape. Each person who left their country experienced a unique departure process. I experienced this as well. The account presented herein is a concise summary of the events that transpired during my difficult and perilous journey to escape, which I vividly recall even after 45 years. It is hoped that these recollections will provide readers with some understanding of the difficult circumstances faced by the Vietnamese people during the significant migration movement of the late 1970s to early 1980s, a period when many sought to leave Vietnam's modern history post-1975.

Contents

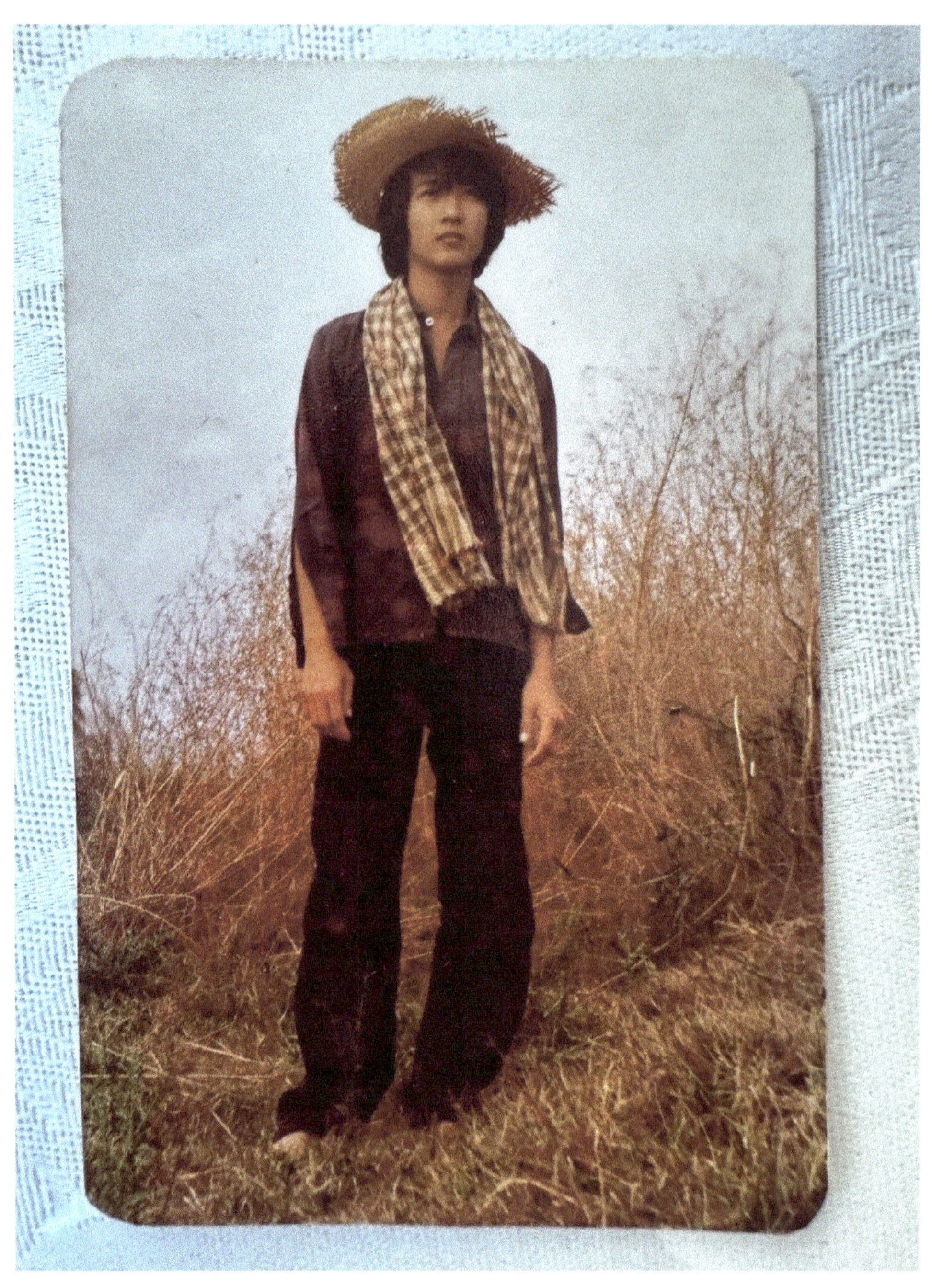

A Cambodian photographer gave me this photo taken when I first moved to Phanat Nikhom camp after living in camp NW9 for five months. Unfortunately, I no longer remember his name. Thank you for providing this valuable photo.

Chapter 1

Chance to Flee and the Final Days in Saigon

I was born into a middle-class family with ten children, including two older sisters and eight brothers. My parents, who worked as traders, earned enough to support us all. We grew up during the war between North and South Vietnam. My parents often sighed and worried about our future as the war between the two regions intensified. Their fears extended beyond survival; they were concerned about how the war might force their children into making unimaginable choices.

The event of April 30, 1975, transformed our entire family's life. The South was defeated, and I had just become a teenager that year. I witnessed soldiers of the Republic of Vietnam (RVN) discard their uniforms on the streets of Saigon. Occasionally, military vehicles carrying North Vietnamese soldiers would kick up dust as they entered the city. My parents' faces were a mix of confusion, joy, and sadness: joy because the country had 'peacefully unified' the North and South, meaning their sons might not have to become soldiers; sadness because they were uncertain about what family life would be like under the new regime. Their mixed emotions reflected the uncertainty that would come to define every decision they made in the years to follow.

Then the inevitable occurred: My parents could no longer conduct business as they had before. Family activities increasingly depleted the money they had saved over many years. Every week, we had to wait in long lines to buy food at government-owned stores. Occasionally, during the week, all the adults in the family were called to participate in the forced labor program. The lives of people living in the country, especially Saigon residents, were increasingly deteriorating. Even for daily meals, many families had started to eat rice mixed with potatoes, corn, and other substitutes.

At the end of 1978, Vietnam invaded Cambodia with the aim of overthrowing the Khmer Rouge regime. Many young men in Saigon, aged 18 and above, were mandatorily drafted to join the military and fight in Cambodia. Fortunately, I was under 18 at that time. However, this luck was overshadowed by the inevitability of what awaited me as I approached the age of conscription. My parents often exchanged anxious glances, knowing they needed to act quickly to protect me from this fate.

In 1979, Vietnam faced two wars: one with Pol Pot's army in Cambodia, bordering southwest Vietnam, and the other with Chinese troops on the Vietnam-China border. The situation was dire for Vietnam: the economy was exhausted, rivers were blocked, and markets were banned. Worst of all, many Vietnamese soldiers lost their lives during that time. My parents' fears grew alongside their exhaustion, and they began to whisper about escape as the only way to secure my future.

Soon, I will reach the age for mandatory military service. My parents were already constantly worried about everything in their daily lives, and now they had to plan my escape. At the beginning of 1979, a very close friend of my parents told them that she was preparing to escape by sea. She said if our family wanted to escape with her, my mother should come to her house to meet the organizer in person and make the payment in gold before the escape.

To meet the appointment, I drove my mother on my Honda to meet and pay the organizer. When we arrived, my mother's friend hugged her and apologized that the organizer couldn't wait and had left half an hour earlier. I felt sad and regretful for missing the opportunity to escape. Before we left, my mother's friend hugged her one last time. They both sobbed, knowing they would never see each other again after decades of doing business together. Her children were also my childhood friends. My mother wished for peace for her friend's family. A few days later, the boat of my mother's friend departed.

Several months passed without any news about the escape. My mother was worried about her friend's family and asked many people about their status. She eventually found out that Pol Pot's navy had sunk their boat off the coast of Cambodia, likely killing the entire family and leading to the confiscation of their house. I was shocked by the news but realized that being half an hour late had saved my life. Haunted by the failed escape of my mother's friend's family, I no longer had any desire to leave the country.

To avoid being drafted into the army, I had to find every way to pass the university entrance exam in 1980. At that time, only about 10% of students were admitted to the university, with half of them being children of high officials of the new regime. Despite the ongoing economic difficulties, my parents still took care of me and prepared me for the college entrance exams. That year was clearly the decisive year of my life.

I met a girl in the same college entrance exam preparation class, but the pressure to get into university was so intense that I didn't dare to focus on dating. If I failed the exam, I would be sent to the army, which would be miserable for both of us.

In early May 1980, I was deeply focused on studying as the exam date approached. Suddenly, my cousin arrived, wanting to discuss something important with my parents. After a few hours of whispering, my parents called me and revealed that they were planning for me to escape again.

Since 1977, I have heard many stories about people escaping the country. The word 'escape' was no longer unfamiliar to me: the lives of Saigon's people were becoming increasingly difficult. Everyone wanted to flee the harsh Communist regime imposed by the Northern government on South Vietnam. As I mentioned earlier, people often joked, 'If a light pole could walk, sooner or later, it would escape!' I had considered escaping many times but had abandoned the idea due to the dangers and high costs involved.

Furthermore, the story of the failed escape plan last year still haunted me. At that time, the average cost for a person to escape from Saigon was about five teals of gold, a significant amount for us. This time, my parents were determined to let me escape because the organizer was my cousin. She had successfully organized several escapes before and now wanted her two younger siblings to escape, so she took charge of the plan. To make more profit and ensure her siblings had relatives to help them, she persuaded my parents to let me join them.

In addition to trusting our relatives to organize the escape, my impending conscription into the army prompted my parents to make a bold decision. Although the war with Cambodia and China had ended in March 1979, the news and images of young soldiers' sacrifices haunted my parents. They realized the urgency of the situation and agreed to let me escape.

My brother, who was two years older, was exempted from military service because he passed the university entrance exam for architecture. However, my parents were most concerned about me. They asked my cousin to give the family a few days to think and make a final decision, as they wanted to hear my opinion directly.

For several days, I was absent-minded and couldn't eat or drink anything. My face, already pale from months of studying for college entrance exams, became even paler. Seeing my condition, my parents hesitated with worry. However, they saw this as a good opportunity to escape, as they trusted my cousin, who had organized several successful escapes. In the end, my parents were determined for me to participate.

I had another brother who was two years younger but much bigger and stronger than me. When he learned about the escape plan, he privately told me that if I went, he would go with me. Knowing that my brother was also willing to take the risk gave me more motivation. We both agreed to leave together.

After learning that my younger brother also wanted to go, my parents seemed even more reluctant. However, seeing my frail appearance, they finally agreed, hoping we could help each other during the escape. After a few days of contemplation, my parents decided to let both of us go together. My cousin mentioned that the escape was expected to take place within a few weeks. Consequently, all my plans for a bright future in college were now completely altered.

While many people typically escaped by sea, our escape was by land. We crossed Cambodia to reach Thailand. Considering the unsuccessful sea escape last year, I considered the land route potentially safer than the sea route.

My brother and I were pretending to be the assistants of the driver who drove the cargo truck carrying rice to supply the Vietnamese soldiers who were defending Cambodia at that time. After several weeks of fighting with Vietnamese soldiers in coordination with the Heng Samrin liberation army, the Khmer Rouge army lost the battle. It withdrew its remnants into the forest along the border between Cambodia and Thailand. Vietnam's rice trucks would depart from Saigon City, run through Go Dau in Tay Ninh province, and then go to Phnom Penh. The last stop was the Sisophon district near the Thailand border.

My brother and I had only a few weeks to prepare. I needed to learn commonly used sentences in English, French, and Cambodian. Despite being ready to escape within this timeframe, I continued to attend school regularly until the last day as a precaution, in case the escape was unsuccessful, allowing me to resume normal classes seamlessly. During these final days of school, I experienced significant worry and found it challenging to concentrate.

After the South was taken over, Saigon faced significant economic challenges. Many people traveled on foot, and owning a bicycle for school was considered fortunate. Crossing the Y-shaped Bridge was difficult due to its steep and lengthy structure. The Tau Hu Canal and the Doi Canal had black water flowing beneath the bridge, with considerable amounts of garbage floating on the surface.

Eagerly waiting for the day to leave, I was ready to leave with the hope of finding a better future. Many families were living in thatched roofs or tin corrugated iron-ramshackle houses on the stilts along the canals. These houses were about to collapse at any moment. How would they live when society got increasingly worse?

But in the end, in retrospect, no matter where I lived, the images of the canals and the bridge commemorating every day I went to school for the years following April 30 were ingrained in my memory and will never fade in my heart.

Despite the numerous tasks that required completion in a limited timeframe before I departed from my hometown, I deemed it essential to bid farewell to two individuals: my girlfriend, who was a classmate, and my best friend, with whom I had maintained a close relationship since ninth grade.

Two days before the planned escape, I met my close friend for coffee and bid farewell. My friend, Dung, expressed his strong desire to escape but was unable to do so due to the recent passing of his father and his mother's deteriorating health. Dung shared that his father had died prematurely in a state of grief and despair amid accusations of being bourgeois, which led to the loss of most of their hard-earned property. I did not disclose the specifics of the land escape, leading Dung to believe that I would be escaping by sea.

May marked the first rainy month of the season each year. That night, the rain was particularly heavy. Dung expressed concern about the possibility of a storm due to the intensity of the rain. I observed the concern on Dung's face. Upon saying farewell, Dung stated that he could only hope for my success on my journey.

The day before my departure, I arranged to meet my girlfriend in the park. To avoid easy identification and present a more age-neutral appearance, I opted to change my hairstyle from a longer style typically associated with students to a shorter style often seen among teenagers. When she noticed my different appearance and unusual behavior, Ngoc seemed surprised and asked about the changes and the reason behind them.

Unable to contain myself, I disclosed my plan to escape tomorrow and implied that it might be our last meeting. Upon hearing this, Ngoc remained silent, staring at me with sorrowful eyes. A few days prior, I had listened to the BBC (British Broadcasting Corporation) radio station and committed to memory the song "Saigon! Farewell." In a subdued voice, I recited, "Saigon, I have lost you in my life... or cried for my lover..."

Ngoc couldn't hold back her tears, and my tears also fell as if wanting to mix with Ngoc's tears.

I experienced profound sadness and emotional turmoil as I prepared to leave my homeland and my beloved, uncertain of whether I would survive or perish. The likelihood of returning seemed remote. Despite my deep affection, I refrained from asking her out due to the daunting challenges I faced. Ultimately, I bid Ngoc farewell with a light kiss on her cheek, believing that we might never meet again.

That night, I had difficulty sleeping. I avoided talking to my parents because I was concerned I might start crying. I spent the night restless, with my mind preoccupied. Part of me was concerned about our escape, and the other part wondered what would happen to our family after we left. Ngoc's tears that afternoon continued to trouble me. My sentiments echoed the lyrics of "*The Heart of a Traveler,*" composed by the late musician Anh Bang: *"I departed from Hanoi at the age of eighteen, just as I had fallen in love. So many beautiful dreams of love turned into smoke and disappeared with the afternoon clouds"*.

Regardless of whether it is Hanoi or Saigon, individuals who leave their hometown experience similar emotions. Saigon, a cherished location, will always remain in my memory, regardless of where I may reside in the world.

Chapter 2

Crossing the Border into Cambodia

As soon as the sun rose, a relative arrived to take my brother and me on a Honda ride. Before we left home, our parents were in tears. They handed each of us a package containing an old set of clothes to disguise ourselves as a driver's assistant, a hat, a pair of sandals, and a bottle of massage oil (used for skin ailments and warmth). A few days earlier, my mother had exchanged two new sets of clothes for two old sets belonging to two regular tricycle riders who frequented our front yard. Additionally, she sewed gold into our hats, shirts, pants, and sandals, advising us to use it if necessary. The fee paid to the escape organizer (our cousin) was five taels each; at that time, 10 taels of gold could purchase a house in Saigon. We paid half upfront, and the remaining half was to be paid upon reaching our destination. According to the plan, once we arrived safely, I was to write a note for the organizer to bring back home, and the rest of the payment would be made. My mother instructed me to write the number 56 on the note if we arrived safely, as my younger brother and I were the sixth and fifth children in our family, respectively.

Otherwise, writing either of the other two numbers would be considered a sign that our trip had been jeopardized.

The relative's task was to drive my brother and me to the Moc Bai border gate in Tay Ninh province, near the border with Cambodia. Beyond that, he was not given any further information. We needed to keep our escape confidential because if discovered, my parents, my brother, and I would be imprisoned. During the journey, our relative inquired if we were "going home," which was slang at the time for "escape". Recognizing that we could no longer hide our intentions, I informed him that we were indeed "going home." Upon reaching the Go Dau district, I requested that our relative allow us to visit our grandmother on our father's side for about an hour.

Go, Dau, was where both of us were born and raised until a few months before the Southern region was invaded. Our grandmother remained there, while our parents' house was adjacent to our grandparents' residence. My grandfather relocated to Saigon, leaving my grandmother alone. Due to our family's move to Saigon, our parents' house was left vacant and quietly closed.

Upon arriving, we parked a Honda in front of our grandmother's house. Upon entering, our grandmother immediately recognized my brother and me as her grandchildren, although she could not recall our names. She inquired about the purpose of our visit, to which I responded that we were in the area for business and took the opportunity to visit her. During that period, many people in Tay Ninh were attempting to escape by land; thus, despite our verbal explanation, it was implicitly understood from her expression that my grandmother knew this was our trip to escape to Thailand via Cambodia.

When my brother and I were young, we frequently visited our grandmother's house, where we enjoyed eating grilled pork with rice paper. Our grandmother was aware of our fondness for this dish; hence, she instructed a child to purchase a tray of grilled pork with rice paper from the nearby restaurant. I became emotional when my grandmother said, "*Enjoy the food you like. You may not have another opportunity to eat it.*" At that moment, I could no longer conceal our escape plan from my grandfather. I had to inform my grandmother that we were on our way to Cambodia. Grandmother embraced her two grandchildren tightly, shed many tears, and wished us success on our journey.

As I gazed upon my parents' house, where my brother and I were born and spent our childhood, I felt a profound sense of sadness. The yard was covered with fallen leaves, dust, and scattered green moss. I pondered whether my parents would retain ownership of their house in the future or if it would be confiscated, like what happened to my friend's family, who were accused of being bourgeois. I recalled the days when my childhood friends and I played marbles together in the front yard. During the annual giant cricket season, we would catch crickets for our mother to cook with rice flour, creating delicious meals for the entire family. Every night, my parents often left a light bulb lit in front of the house so that we could catch crickets with neighborhood children. I wondered about the current lives of my childhood friends; perhaps they had joined the military or escaped, as I did. My contemplation was suddenly interrupted by a relative who informed us that time was limited and we needed to proceed to Moc Bai. We mounted the Honda and set off.

The Honda traversed the Go Dau Bridge, which was situated a few hundred meters from my grandmother's residence. This bridge extended over the Vam Co Dong River and had suffered significant deterioration due to being mined several times during the war. Traversing the bridge required caution as there was a risk of falling into the water.

My maternal grandparents' house was located near the base of the bridge. While the coconut tree, star fruit tree, and mango tree remained, our grandparents passed away. The responsibility of maintaining their house had been entrusted to our uncle.

During my youth, I frequently delivered my mother's cooked meals to our elderly grandparents, who no longer desired to cook. I enjoyed these trips, as they often resulted in receiving delicious candies from my grandparents. Although these memories seem small, they resonate deeply with me now, evoking feelings of sadness. Perhaps this is because I feel that I am about to lose them and may never see them again.

On the other side of the bridge, two canals ran parallel to both sides of the road. Historically, during the high-water season, I frequently accompanied my uncles to fish for perch there. The continuous stretches of rivers and rice fields flanking the road evoked a deep appreciation for my birthplace. At that time, the Go Dau district was economically underdeveloped; however, it possessed a distinctive charm and beauty.

The scenery along both sides of the road was chaotic and swirling, imprinting itself in my mind. Shortly thereafter, we arrived at Moc Bai, where about five trucks were already parked, awaiting their turn to cross the border gate. Our relative introduced us to the driver for whom my brother and I would act as assistants. It turned out that the driver was our cousin's husband. He was a Vietnamese individual who had previously resided in Cambodia and returned to Vietnam in 1970 during the "Cap Duon" movement (the Cambodian movement to purge the Vietnamese). He spoke both Vietnamese and Cambodian fluently. After introducing us to the truck driver, our relative bid us farewell turned around on his Honda, and headed back to Saigon.

At that time, my brother and I were unable to cross the border gate controlled by the border guards properly. Inside the truck, there were two genuine driver's assistants assigned to present the necessary documents, facilitating the delivery of food to the Vietnamese soldiers in Cambodia. Each vehicle was permitted to have two driver's assistants. Once we successfully crossed the border, my brother and I would replace the two legitimate driver's assistants, who would then assume the guise of Cambodians. These two driver's assistants were Vietnamese and proficient in speaking Cambodian.

As previously arranged, my brother and I were transported across the border by a local individual on a two-wheeled Honda motorcycle through numerous rice fields. After approximately thirty minutes, we arrived at a truck station in Cambodia, where we were transferred to the vehicle of my cousin's husband.

Subsequently, we changed into the attire that our parents had provided us upon our departure from Saigon.

My brother and I assumed the roles of driver's assistants while the actual driver's assistants disguised themselves as Cambodians. Approximately 20 Cambodian individuals were already hitchhiking on top of the truck. During that period, Cambodia was experiencing significant poverty, particularly in terms of limited transportation options. Consequently, whenever people spotted a vehicle, they would request a ride. Thus, it was common to see around 10 to 20 Cambodians hitchhiking on the top of trucks. The two assistants now pretended to be Cambodians and integrated themselves into the group.

The cargo truck continued its journey and went through multiple checkpoints. Vietnamese soldiers and Heng Samrin soldiers staffed each checkpoint. The Vietnamese soldiers inspected the vehicle documents and the goods on the vehicle while the Heng Samrin soldiers checked Cambodians who were hitchhiking. Due to thorough preparation, we passed through many checkpoints with minimal issues.

After about four years (1975-1979) under Pol Pot's genocidal regime, Cambodia had improved slowly. It was poor and had almost nothing left. Some Cambodian hitchhikers on the truck who could speak Vietnamese told me many stories about the cruel killing of people by the Khmer Rouge regime controlled by Pol Pot. The Cambodian people were pleased when Vietnamese soldiers liberated them.

During our journey, when we felt hungry, we parked the truck on the roadside and utilized a portion of the rice from the cargo to prepare a meal. Given the significant quantity of rice the truck was transported, using a small amount was negligible. Additionally, we bartered rice for dried fish to complement our meal. The roadsides were typically deserted, with minimal vehicular traffic; only the occasional military vehicle and sporadic bicycles could be seen. Pedestrians were common along both sides of the road. Much of the surrounding land was left uncultivated and abandoned.

With about two hours left to reach the capital, Phnom Penh, it was already dark. Although Pol Pot was defeated, the remnants of their army were still hiding in unknown locations, so driving at night was not safe; the driver decided to rest on this side of the river and then the next morning take a ferry to cross the river and continue driving. The Cambodian hitchhikers automatically got off the truck and dispersed.

The following morning, the driver, his two assistants, my brother, and I awoke to prepare breakfast. I offered to wash the dishes by the riverbank. Cambodia's reputation as a land abundant in fish proved accurate: as soon as leftover grains of rice fell into the water, numerous fish quickly gathered and competed for them. Remarkably, even the soap bubbles were consumed by the fish. Once our tasks were completed, the five of us boarded the truck and resumed our journey to Phnom Penh.

Approximately an hour before reaching Phnom Penh, the driver halted the truck to ensure that everything was in order before reporting to the station. Believing all was well, he proceeded to start the vehicle. However, one of the assistants was still on the roof, and when the truck moved, he fell onto the asphalt road, losing consciousness. Consequently, the driver stopped the truck and called for an ambulance to transport the injured assistant to the hospital.

My brother and I were extremely concerned and fearful. If the assistant sustained severe injuries, our mission would be compromised as there would not be enough assistants to return to Vietnam. Subsequently, the driver accompanied the injured assistant to the hospital via ambulance. Meanwhile, the second assistant, my brother, and I remained behind to watch over the truck. We could only hope for a positive outcome.

Two hours later, the ambulance returned. I immediately approached it. Fortunately, the injured assistant sustained only a broken arm, which was properly bandaged. Had such an incident occurred to me, I may not have fared as well, considering the significant height of the fall from the truck's hood onto the asphalt road.

Our truck proceeded through the checkpoint in Phnom Penh. By then, it was too late for lunch, and everyone was hungry. We agreed to eat separately and reconvened 60 minutes later. My brother and I headed to a nearby market. In Phnom Penh, the capital, life appeared more vibrant than in the suburban areas we had recently traveled through. Fortunately, some individuals at the market spoke Vietnamese. My brother and I approached a Vietnamese food stand and placed our order. However, the Vietnamese vendor informed us that the Cambodian Government had recently changed its currency: the Riel of the old regime was no longer valid. To purchase food, we needed to pay in gold or the new Riel currency. Surprised and uncertain of what to do, we realized we had forgotten to bring the new Riel. Using gold to pay could expose us as attempting to escape. As we stood there awkwardly, the vendor smiled sympathetically and whispered in Vietnamese, "*It's okay. You two can eat. I feel sorry for you. I won't take any money.*" Grateful, we quickly ate our meal, thanked her hesitantly, and promptly returned to the meeting place.

Within four years, Cambodia underwent two regime changes, resulting in significant turmoil for its citizens. During this period, the lives of Cambodians were extremely chaotic. As an individual who had secretly fled and was unfamiliar with the Cambodian language, I experienced considerable anxiety. I pondered over the potential challenges that lay ahead in the journey.

After lunch, we promptly departed from Phnom Penh with the objective of reaching Battambang City before nightfall. Along both sides of the road, remnants of the recent conflict between Pol Pot's forces and Vietnamese troops, along with Heng Samrin's liberation army, were still visible. As we traveled further west towards the Thai border, the landscape became increasingly desolate and tragic. The checkpoints grew more stringent, and the soldiers conducted thorough inspections and interrogations. However, due to meticulous preparation, we successfully arrived in Battambang City. We stayed overnight in Battambang and proceeded to Sisophon town the following morning. Sisophon is the final small town on Cambodia's western boundary before crossing into Thai territory. Vietnamese soldiers were heavily stationed at posts along the border. Our vehicle was tasked with delivering rice to this area as part of its mission.

Sisophon town was not far from Battambang city, and we anticipated arriving before noon. The driver informed my brother and me that there was one final checkpoint before entering Sisophon. This station was known for its strictness and thorough inspections. As our truck approached the station, my heart began to pound, and my brother appeared equally anxious. Unlike previous stations where Vietnamese soldiers merely requested our documents and inspected the truck, this time, they interrogated the driver's assistants in Cambodian. I sat still, my entire body trembling, as I had not expected the Vietnamese border guards to speak Cambodian. It seemed that due to the high number of Vietnamese people escaping by land during that period, stricter controls were necessary. Fortunately, after a few minutes of questioning, the border guards allowed our truck to pass through the station. We felt grateful for the smooth passage.

We arrived in Sisophon around noon, and the driver dropped my brother and me off at the market. The driver and his assistants proceeded to deliver rice to the Vietnamese army garrison. Unlike Phnom Penh, we were unable to find anyone who spoke Vietnamese, requiring my brother and me to use gestures when purchasing food.

A small market was situated near a pond, which served multiple purposes, from bathing cattle to providing water for cooking and drinking. Despite the visibly unsanitary conditions, our hunger compelled us to buy some food. Transactions here required payment in gold. I used a gold piece hidden in my hat to pay for the food. The saleswoman weighed the gold and then cut off a small portion of it.

In general, due to the potential danger associated with exposure to Vietnamese soldiers, we endeavored to minimize our contact with the surrounding populace.

After our meal, my brother and I proceeded to the designated meeting location and waited. Shortly thereafter, following the delivery of the rice, the truck returned to collect us. The truck halted at the parking area, where I observed several trucks that I had previously seen in Moc Bai. The driver informed us that we needed to remain concealed in the truck until late afternoon, after which we would depart along with four other individuals. I surmised that those four individuals likely arrived similarly as we did.

It was late in the afternoon when four young men from nearby trucks discreetly entered our vehicle. It transpired that two of these individuals were our cousins, who were also siblings of the organizer. The other two young men were of Cho Lon Chinese (Vietnamese of Chinese origin residing in the Cho Lon area near Saigon). The driver, who was my cousin's husband, drove the truck to a rice field outside the town. Upon our arrival at the field, we encountered a Cambodian man approximately 40 years of age who had been awaiting our arrival. After exchanging a few sentences in Cambodian with the man, the driver gestured for us to disembark and follow the Cambodian man, who did not speak Vietnamese. The six of us remained silent and attentively followed his instructions. The truck then returned to Sisophon town. I reflected on the impending journey, anticipating that it would be more perilous than the past few days.

Chapter 3

In the heart of Sisophon Forest

We found ourselves surrounded by numerous abandoned rice fields, now overgrown with bushes, with only a small path available for passage. We proceeded along this trail. After approximately 20 minutes of walking, our guide signaled us to exercise caution as we approached within about 100 meters of a concealed fort. I surmised it was a guard post manned by Vietnamese border guards. It appeared to be dinnertime, as smoke was emanating from the post, likely from the soldiers' cooking activities. We quietly made our way past, taking advantage of their preoccupation with meal preparation. Consequently, we successfully bypassed the first guard post. Proceeding further, we encountered a second post. As we were still on the trail and a considerable distance from the fort, we managed to pass it without incident.

The guide signaled that there remained one final post. The sky had already darkened by that time. Unlike the preceding two posts, this one was approximately 20 meters from our trail. I could distinctly hear the soldiers conversing in Vietnamese while dining. Interspersed with their conversation was the sound of traditional singing emanating from the radio. Due to the proximity of this guard post, we needed to exercise extreme caution while passing. It seemed meticulously planned that our passage through this post would occur at night, as it would be exceptionally challenging to evade detection otherwise. The guide instructed us to remove our sandals and continue barefoot, requiring us to walk slowly to reduce noise.

As we walked past the post, a flashlight beam unexpectedly illuminated it. Fortunately, the light shined on the ground rather than directly at us. Upon seeing the flashlight, our guide promptly signaled for us to take cover in the nearby dense bushes. Within moments, we were all concealed among the foliage.

It became evident that the soldier who had used the flashlight had stepped out to urinate. During this time, he intermittently directed the flashlight in our direction, causing considerable anxiety. I experienced heightened fear. My heart nearly ceased to beat. One could ponder if it was a stroke of fortune or some inexplicable force that kept us undetected despite being only approximately 20 meters away from the soldier. After completing his task, the soldier returned to the post without raising any alarms. The guide appeared relieved, indicating that there were no further guard posts along our path.

Upon putting my sandals back on and resuming my walk, I noticed that my left foot was bleeding and experiencing significant pain. Due to the darkness at that time, I was unable to determine what I had stepped on, and to this day, the cause remains unclear. When I jumped into the bush, possibly out of fear, I did not initially feel any pain. Despite the discomfort, I endeavored to endure the pain and continued walking to rejoin the group.

Aware that we would not come across any additional guard posts, our group of seven proceeded at a normal pace. Upon reaching the forest's edge, darkness enveloped us, yet the moonlight provided just enough illumination to discern the surrounding landscape. The guide then led us along a trail, taking us further and further into the forest.

It was late at night, approximately around 11 pm or midnight. Due to fatigue and hunger, we were considering asking our guide for a stop when it began to rain. The guide located an abandoned thatched hut nearby where we could take shelter from the rain. The rainfall persisted overnight, resulting in cold temperatures experienced by all individuals. We sat close together to maintain warmth. While most seemed able to endure the conditions temporarily, I struggled due to cold, fatigue, hunger, and a foot injury that caused me to shiver uncontrollably. Observing my condition, my brother handed me a bottle of massage oil from his bag. After applying the oil, my shaking persisted. My brother then retrieved another bottle of massage oil from my bag. Without any further hesitation, I risked my life and drank the entire second bottle! Maybe I was not destined to die. About five minutes later, my shaking stopped. I asked to sit in the middle of six people to get the warmest temperature and then fell asleep...

*

As dawn approached, the rain from the previous night had ceased. The guide roused everyone to proceed further into the forest. Occasionally, individuals were observed traveling in the opposite direction, either walking or pushing bicycles laden with bulky goods. It appeared they were transporting Thai products for sale in Cambodia or Vietnam. During my time in Vietnam, I frequently assisted my older sister with the purchase and sale of Thai goods in Saigon.

We proceeded in the direction indicated by the guide. As we advanced, the forest grew increasingly dense. Everyone experienced hunger and fatigue. At approximately 9 or 10 am, the guide halted and instructed us to continue along the trail with the smugglers while he returned. This change caused significant fear and frustration among us, as we felt abandoned in the middle of the forest. However, there was no alternative. We had to persevere silently and proceed because returning would pose an even greater danger due to the potential capture by Vietnamese soldiers.

The guide departed, leaving us akin to a vessel adrift in the vast ocean without a captain. We continued along the winding forest trail. My left foot was causing significant pain, hindering my ability to keep pace with the others in our group. Consequently, it was not long before the four individuals began to distance themselves from my brother and me.

Uncertain of what lay ahead, my brother and I proceeded in silence. When we encountered some smugglers along the trail, I inquired about the direction to

Thailand. Prior to our escape, I had learned a few phrases in Cambodian: "tau" for going, "tau na" for going where, and "tau Siam" for going to Thailand. Therefore, each time we encountered someone, I would say "Tau Siam," and they would indicate the appropriate direction.

Each time we met individuals involved in smuggling, we inquired about the directions to Thailand. I reasoned that continuous inquiries would eventually lead us there. When we experienced hunger, we either requested food or utilized gold to purchase it. In both instances, they either provided or sold it to us. Approximately an hour after being abandoned by our guide, we found ourselves completely disoriented in the dense forest. Then, I observed two soldiers in the distance carrying firearms. As we approached, they aimed their weapons at us. With expressions of serious intent, the soldiers demanded sternly, "Tau na." Recognizing the potential danger posed by their firearms, we responded promptly and respectfully, "Tau Siam." Upon stating our intention to travel to Thailand, the soldiers' expressions appeared to soften. After scrutinizing us for a while, they proceeded to speak entirely in Cambodian. We could not understand anything. But looking at their clothes, I guessed that they were the remnants of Pol Pot's army. My brother and I were extremely scared. I remember when we were sitting on the hood of the truck on the way here, the hitchhikers told us about the brutal murders of the Pol Pot regime: After losing the battle, they retreated to the forest between the border of Thailand and Cambodia. Perhaps it was because of such a situation that the guide did not enter the forest and left us before facing the Pol Pot soldiers!

Aware that my brother and I were Vietnamese individuals attempting to escape, the Pon Pot soldiers promptly confiscated our hats, shirts, and sandals. It appears they had previously taken possessions from other escapees as well. They stripped things that they thought would have gold hidden in them. Luckily, they didn't take away our pants: My brother's pants didn't have any gold in them, but mine did. Two Pol Pot soldiers threw their old shirts back to us and sent us on our way. The gold in the hat, shirt and sandals were robbed. Despite our mutual fear and sadness, we had to proceed. Without sandals, my left foot sustained an increased injury and began to swell.

Around noon, after some additional walking, we arrived at a location with a considerable gathering of people. It was revealed to be a small market situated within the forest. The market comprised several huts offering food, water, and miscellaneous items. Surprised by the sudden commotion, my brother and I felt hungry and fatigued, but we were uncertain about procuring lunch. While we were struggling to search for food, a Pol Pot soldier unexpectedly showed up, pointed a gun at us and forced us into the guard station next to the market.

Upon arriving at the station, my brother and I unexpectedly encountered three individuals from our escape group: one was our cousin, and the other two were friends from Cho Lon Chinese. However, our other cousin was absent, and his whereabouts were unknown. At that time, we were confined together in a single location. The station where the five of us were detained was small, staffed by only a few Pol Pot soldiers. No one on either side spoke or understood each other... but our group was as large as the Pol Pot soldiers in the station, so they were also afraid that we might cause a riot. Therefore, they guarded very carefully: They always had guns ready to shoot, and they kept knives in their hands. One time, a Pol Pot soldier approached me with a sickle knife and raised it to cut my throat. He moved the knife back and forth across my neck a few times, but he didn't cut. I was afraid that I would pee in my pants! But then he lowered the knife and smiled triumphantly. Maybe he wanted to scare me or for some unknown reason that prevented him from killing me…

Feeling anxious, I lowered my head in uncertainty about our future. Suddenly, a woman's voice caught my attention. When I glanced up, I noticed a woman in her 40s moving purposefully around the station. After conversing with the station chief, she indicated that she was the guide's wife and then proceeded to purchase food for us. As we were all quite hungry, the five of us ate promptly.

After we finished our meal, the guide's wife provided me with a piece of paper and a pen, indicating that I should write a note confirming our safe arrival. This note was to be taken back to Vietnam to secure the remaining half of the gold. At that moment, it became clear to me that she had informed the Pol Pot soldiers to detain us in order to claim the rest of the gold. It is plausible that there was only one trail through that part of the forest, which we must have traversed. Regarding her husband, his decision to abandon us in the jungle likely stemmed from his fear of confronting the Pol Pot soldiers.

Holding the pen, tears fell from my eyes: If I wrote that Pol Pot soldiers captured us, our parents would surely die of despair. How could I write that we arrived safely while, in front of my eyes, there were four or five Pol Pot soldiers pointing guns at us and ready to shoot at any moment. Even though they didn't tie us up, they treated us like war prisoners!

Looking at my brother's innocent face full of fear, I felt extremely sad. Just because he wanted to follow me, he was now suffering like this! And maybe after I finished writing the letter, they would smash our heads like they killed Cambodians during the four years under Pol Pot's genocide regime. I knew that they hated Vietnamese people very much. I wondered if this was a letter of suicide or not.

Hesitating and uncertain about what to write, I found myself overcome with tears of despair and panic. Observing my distress, the guide's wife approached me and spoke a few reassuring words in Cambodian, "*Ot e te.*" Although I did not understand the meaning at the time, her sincerity was evident. Reflecting on the presence of the organizer's brothers during this escape, I felt a glimmer of hope.

I recalled my parents mentioning that my cousin had successfully organized several escapes previously.

Summoning my resolve, I wrote on the piece of paper: *"The road is arduous and dangerous, but we have arrived."* Next, I needed to inscribe the code to the paper. My parents had instructed me to write "56" if it was truly safe, otherwise to write a different number. Despite feeling that success was unlikely, I lowered my pen and wrote "56". Closing my eyes, I whispered to myself, "Let fate decide."

The guide's spouse took the document I had just completed and promptly departed. Two soldiers from the group of Pol Pot forces signaled for us to leave the station and follow them. A Pol Pot soldier led the way, followed by the five of us, with another soldier at the rear. My left foot continued to ache, causing me to lag behind the rest of the group. None of the five of us possessed hats or sandals anymore. Although we reunited at the station, there was no opportunity to inquire further. I guessed that perhaps the other three people had also been robbed, similar to my brother and myself.

Two Pol Pot soldiers extradited five of us, and we quietly followed. The two sides did not understand each other's language at all. We only heard their voices saying "tau," and we followed their command even, not knowing where they were going.

The trail was significantly muddy due to yesterday's rain. Unfortunately, none of the five of us had any sandals, so we were compelled to walk barefoot, which proved to be quite challenging. The lead Pol Pot soldier, along with the rest of us, maintained a brisk pace. My left foot was particularly swollen and painful, yet I had to persist through the discomfort as the rear Pol Pot soldier constantly aimed his gun at me while urging me to move faster. The increasing distance between us forced the group at the front to stop periodically and wait for me to catch up.

After walking for over an hour, my cousin needed to pee. The leading soldier pointed to the bushes beside the trail, indicating permission was granted. He also carefully indicated for us to be cautious of landmines. I recalled hearing on television in Saigon that when Pol Pot's forces retreated into the forest, they placed numerous mines and traps to hinder the progress of Vietnamese soldiers. My cousin finished and returned to the group, quietly mentioning that he saw a dead body lying in the bushes. Upon hearing this, we all felt concerned about what might lie ahead on our journey.

The group continued walking for approximately three hours, during which time everyone experienced fatigue, hunger, and thirst. I was particularly distressed due to significant pain and swelling in my left foot. My gait had become abnormal, resembling that of someone with a disability, yet I persevered through the discomfort and continued walking, motivated by the hope of survival. There was a time when four people in the group and the leading Pol Pot soldier were far away from me and the rear soldier. The soldier in the rear had to call out to the soldier in the front to stop and wait, but the soldier in the front couldn't hear him, so he had to fire a warning shot. Upon hearing the loud gunshot, I was startled and fell into the mud. My brother, who was ahead of me, looked back and saw me lying in the mud, mistakenly believing that I had been shot. He shouted, *"Dead! Brother Fifth has been shot!"*

All four people in the group were terrified. I tried to stand up and continue walking slowly... but at this point, I really couldn't walk anymore. I just kept wiggling. Seeing this painful situation, my brother could not help it anymore. He had to go back and stand by my shoulder to help me continue. Then, the two brothers unsteadily walked in despair. I saw my brother's feet, which were also swollen because he had been walking in the forest for more than five hours with bare feet since the Pol Pot soldiers robbed our sandals.

We still had no idea where these two Pol Pot soldiers wanted to take us. If they wanted to kill us, they wouldn't have needed to waste time and effort to keep us going for more than a few hours...With the only faint hope that they wouldn't kill us, for survival, we just had to keep obeying their commands.

The two Pol Pot soldiers, accustomed to forest life, each carried a canteen and a bag of dry rice. In contrast, we were exhausted, hungry, and thirsty. As we struggled along the trail, a Cambodian woman approached and offered me water from her canteen, saying, "Drink, dear" in Vietnamese. I was as astonished as if I had been revived from near death. When I inquired how she knew Vietnamese, she explained that she had lived in Vietnam during her youth. Despite having only a few sips of water left in her canteen, I asked what she would drink after giving it to me. She reassured me that it was not an issue, as she would reach a stream within five or six minutes where she could refill her bottle.

After drinking a few sips of water, I felt a little stronger. I expressed my gratitude and returned the empty bottle to her. She promptly left, avoiding any interaction with Pol Pot soldiers. As she departed, she spoke two sentences in Vietnamese and Cambodian: *"It's okay, ot e te."* It was then that I understood the meaning of what the guide's wife had previously said: *"It's okay."* Hearing this, we suddenly felt a sense of relief and happiness, which gave us the energy to continue walking. Indeed, about six minutes later, we reached a stream. The two Pol Pot soldiers washed their faces and refilled their canteens while the five of us also washed our faces and drank as much water as possible.

Hearing the words *"It's okay, ot e te"* from the old woman, the five of us acted as if we had been rescued from a state of despair. We began to see a glimmer of hope for survival ahead. We accepted ourselves as prisoners of war and quietly followed the two Pol Pot soldier's commands.

Chapter 4
A Life Extinguished in a Heartbeat

Despite having the opportunity to wash my face and refresh myself, I remained unsteady on my feet. I quietly asked my brother, "Brother Sixth, could you assist me with walking, please?" We addressed each other by our birth order at home; I was the fifth sibling, and he was the sixth. Without a word, my brother supported me as we walked. Observing his weary expression, it was evident that he, too, was exhausted, yet he exerted every effort to aid me. I felt deeply sympathetic for both of us. The other group of three people maintained a lead ahead of us, stopping only when the distance between us grew too large, allowing us to catch up. By observing the sky and following the sunlight, I deduced that we were heading west through the forest. Before our escape, I had learned to navigate using the sun. The forest straddled the border between Cambodia and Thailand, and by continuing westward, we would eventually reach Thailand.

From morning until now, I have not observed any birds or encountered any wild animals, nor have I discovered any fruit-bearing trees. The forest in this area primarily consists of tree species that are like the oil tree native to Vietnam. Occasionally, we encountered a few individuals moving in the opposite direction from us. They walked past, glanced at us, and then proceeded on their way without engaging in conversation. They were likely apprehensive about interacting with soldiers loyal to Pol Pot. From time to time, we heard distant explosions, possibly caused by someone inadvertently stepping on a landmine. This prompted me to reflect on the precarious nature of human life in the forest.

It was getting into the late afternoon. And we were hungry, thirsty and very tired. As for me, my left foot from the accident was constantly swollen, and I felt even more tired than anyone else. I was almost exhausted: If I kept going like this, I would probably faint in a few hours. The two Pol Pot soldiers kept pointing their guns at us and kept saying "*tau*." I remember that before the escape, my parents told me that, if necessary, I should take out the gold hidden in my belongings and use it. Knowing that I could not go any further, I intended to take the gold out of the hem of my pants and give it to the two Pol Pot soldiers in exchange for food, water, and rest. The gold was sewn into the hem of my pants so that I couldn't get it out. I quickly asked my cousin to let me borrow some gold, and I will return it later. He was also hungry and tired, so he agreed. He took a necklace out of his pants and gave it to me. I gave the necklace to the rear Pol Pot soldier and gestured to him that we needed to eat and rest. He took the necklace but didn't say a word, just gestured to us to keep going.

After about five minutes, two Pol Pot soldiers stopped and pointed to a puddle of water on the side of the trail and gestured to us to drink. The water appeared as dark as coffee, and none of us dared to consume it. However, my thirst and exhaustion were too overwhelming for me to resist, so I decided to drink it despite the potential consequences. Immediately after I had finished drinking, I was prompted to continue moving. The water seemed to provide me with some strength that facilitated my walking, though my brother still had to assist me. At this juncture, I observed that my brother was also very fatigued. We both proceeded slowly while the pain in my foot was excruciating.

After advancing for another half hour, two Pol Pot soldiers stopped at a guard post that two other Pol Pot soldiers guarded. They exchanged a few words, and then, two Pol Pot soldiers at the checkpoint took out a pot of leftover rice and a plate with a few slices of leftover dried fish. The five of us gathered and quickly ate the food. The food was all gone quickly! The Pol Pot soldiers forced us to continue... It was about late six o'clock in the afternoon...

We walked for about another hour. The sunlight began to dim. The forest around us was still dense. Everyone was tired on their last breath. As for me, I was completely exhausted. I fell to the ground. My brother burst into tears. He shouted, "*Brother Fifth is about to die!*". Hearing my brother's scream and seeing me falling and rolling on the ground, the other three people in the group ran back. Then, they decided to take turns helping me walk. The two Pol Pot soldiers still said nothing, stood by and watched. They kept urging us to move on. Their guns were always pointing at us.

We kept walking for a while. Even though I was exhausted, I was still awake. Seeing the unsteady steps of my brother, my cousin, and the two Cho Lon Chinese who took turns helping me walk, I felt guilty. It was just because of me that everyone had to suffer so much. The pain in my foot was too much, and I couldn't bear it. I thought I no longer had the strength to walk anymore, writhing like a dying person. I could not speak anymore. I decided to sacrifice. I gestured to everyone to go ahead and leave me in the middle of the forest. If I had to die, it would be only me!

The other three people saw that the situation could no longer be resolved, so they decided to leave me behind. My brother couldn't bear to leave me alone. He used all his remaining strength to drag me along. He was determined to stay with me to the end! The other three and two Pol Pot soldiers continued walking and left me and my brother behind.

Then, they gradually moved away from us. Summoning all my remaining strength, I attempted to signal to my brother to leave me behind and pursue the others. Otherwise, we might both perish in the middle of the forest, which would be a regrettable loss. I endeavored to lift my face to see my brother one last time. In a moment of despair, I suddenly noticed a distant light and tried to direct my finger towards it. Observing the direction indicated by my gesture, my brother also spotted the light. Unable to contain himself, he exclaimed, "*There is a light!*"

At that time, the three in our group and the two Pol Pot soldiers were only about 30 meters away from us. And the voice in the forest echoed far away. Hearing my brother's screams, they stopped and looked in the direction my brother was pointing. Even though it was almost completely dark, they probably could have seen the light, too. Everyone was happy, as if we were about to drown, but grabbed a life buoy. Then, the three ran back with my brother. They all took turns carrying me forward. Oh! No one could confirm whether that magical light was real or just an illusion... but right now, it was clearly a ray of hope during despair!

That light was naturally like a source of life, giving us more motivation. Everyone tried to mobilize their last strength to carry me forward. About 20 minutes later, we arrived at a place where many leaf huts and Pol Pot soldiers were working with military equipment in the middle of the jungle. Two Pol Pot soldiers escorted us to a tree nearby and told us to rest there. As for me, I fell to the ground and passed out immediately.

*

The following morning, I awoke feeling somewhat improved, although my left foot remained swollen and painful. My brother and the other three members of our group had risen earlier. Upon noticing that I was awake, my brother inquired quietly, "*Are you alright, Brother Fifth? I feared you might not survive the night.*" I responded, "*I am feeling better, though my left foot is still in pain. Without your assistance, I likely would have succumbed to exhaustion.*"

Leaning my back against the tree, I tried to close my eyes to calm down but could not fall asleep. The events of the past two days persistently occupied my thoughts. While in a state between wakefulness and sleep, I heard a soft voice calling me, "*Brother, brother.*" Upon opening my eyes and looking toward the source of the voice, I noticed a young man seated a few meters away. I had not observed his arrival... Noticing that I was now awake, he inquired, *"Were all of you brought here last night?"*

I remained silent and simply nodded. He mentioned that he, too, had been brought here the previous afternoon. Realizing he was in the same situation as me, I felt reassured and initiated a conversation with him.

He mentioned that he was a Tra Vinh Khmer, a Vietnamese of Khmer origin residing in Tra Vinh province, Vietnam. His family faced financial difficulties, and he was on the verge of being drafted into the Vietnamese army, prompting him to escape. He was fluent in both Vietnamese and Cambodian. I informed him that I was a 12th-grade student preparing for the university entrance exam and that there was an escape plan organized by my cousin, whom my parents highly trusted. He told me that because he could speak Cambodian fluently, he learned a lot of valuable information from the Pol Pot soldiers. He said, "*We are so lucky. If we had come here a few months ago, we would have all been killed!*". He added that when the Pol Pot army lost the battle, the remnants of the army fled into the forest. They did not have enough food to eat, all aid came from China. But because the aids were not enough, their lives were horrible.

On the other hand, they hated Vietnam very much. At that time, if they saw anyone who was Vietnamese, they would kill them. Later, thanks to the International Red Cross, they intervened by setting specific conditions: every Vietnamese as a refugee, the International Red Cross could exchange 40 bags of rice.

Now I understood why yesterday the Pol Pot soldier already pressed the knife to my neck and then took the knife back. In addition, they walked day and night to bring us here. The Tra Vinh Khmer friend added that in a few days, they would transfer the people being locked up there to a concentration camp...I glanced at the surrounding landscape and knew that place was a military zone...

We conversed quietly for a short period before ceasing communication entirely. I then leaned against the tree, closed my eyes, and wished to erase the memories of the past few days.

I was hungry, and others in our group might have been as well. Around noon, Pol Pot soldiers brought rice and salt for us to eat. After eating, I went to the tree to rest again.

That afternoon, while everyone was sitting under the trees, I saw a group of Pol Pot soldiers coming toward us. They made us line up. My Tra Vinh Khmer friend stood near me. A leader in the group of Pol Pot soldiers came to check on each of us. Coming toward me, he suddenly shouted *"te hien. te hien!"*. Right after, the Pol Pot soldiers forced me down. I did not understand anything: Why were people in the same group okay but not me?

The leader gestured to me to take off my pants and hand them to him. I was now only wearing shorts and a tattered shirt. As soon as he finished checking, he ordered his soldiers to tie me up. Just as I was being tied up, I suddenly remembered that my Tra Vinh Khmer friend was standing next to me who could speak Cambodian. I quickly asked for help, *"Brother, please ask them why they tied me up."* Feeling so pitiful, he started speaking Cambodian to some of Pol Pot's soldiers. Then he explained to me: *"The leader discovered that your pants were those of Vietnamese soldiers. They suspected you as a Vietnamese spy mixing in with the escaping people."* I felt like I was struck by lightning. I froze! It was surprising to find out that the trousers worn by the tricycle driver in front of our house were, in fact, Vietnamese army pants. The presence of these distinctive pants posed a serious threat to my safety. I promptly informed my Tra Vinh Khmer friend that, to disguise myself as the driver's assistant effectively, I had swapped my new attire for the driver's older garments in front of our residence in Saigon. He listened attentively and remained silent, gazing at the ground.

I earnestly requested his assistance once more. Although he genuinely believed in my situation, his fear prevented him from acting. He remained silent, unable to speak further.

Pressed to the ground, I couldn't see anything. In that moment of despair, I suddenly heard a few Cambodian words coming from the Tra Vinh Khmer friend. I did not know what he said to them. Then, a few minutes later, the leader came to look at me again. This time, he grabbed my hair and looked at my face, scrutinizing it very carefully. After glaring, he spoke *"che chien"* and then ordered his men to untie me. He threw my Vietnamese military pants into a bush nearby, then grabbed an old pair of pants drying nearby, threw them back at me and then left.

After all of Pol Pot's soldiers had departed, I regained my composure and expressed gratitude to my Tra Vinh Khmer friend. I inquired about the meanings of *"te hien"* and *"che chien."* He explained that *"te hien"* refers to a soldier and *"che chien"* means a civilian. This clarification helped me understand why I was spared; it was due to the explanations provided by my Tra Vinh Khmer friend. I am truly thankful for this blessing.

*

Like prisoners of war, we all sat near the trees and bowed our heads. No one talked to anyone, just like that. Time passed slowly, and we felt like we had given up everything, not knowing what else to do; no matter what happened, it would happen.

Just like lunch, dinner that day consisted of a small portion of rice and some salt. After eating, the two Cho Lon Chinese friends sat close and conversed. My brother sat alone, staring into space, his thoughts unknown. It is possible that he was experiencing homesickness or feeling remorse about his departure. I also wondered about my cousin and the thoughts of others. My cousin's face showed signs of sadness and worry, possibly concerned for his missing brother since the guide abandoned us. I was afraid of the possibility that the Pol Pot soldiers might return. I regretted that the pants with hidden gold had been discarded nearby. All our gold had been robbed, and only some remained in those pants, now thrown into a bush about 20 meters away from me. My mind kept wandering. The sun had set, but I hadn't noticed.

That night, I remained awake until very late, unable to rest peacefully. I was distressed by the near-fatal incident that occurred in the afternoon. Additionally, I regretted losing the gold in my possession. In the late afternoon, the sadness and anxiety displayed by my cousin deeply affected me. I reflected on my fortunate circumstances of still having my brother while my cousin's brother was missing. I also wondered if my cousin still had any remaining gold. I had borrowed a necklace from him yesterday to gain permission for food and drink, although I only managed to consume a few sips of water resembling black coffee and a small portion of leftover rice. This sustenance provided just enough energy to continue walking a little further, which ultimately proved to be a matter of life and death. I am grateful for my cousin's generosity in lending me the necklace: without the water and rice that night, I might have succumbed to exhaustion before seeing the light.

I continued to experience restlessness until late into the night. Everyone around me was exhausted and eventually fell asleep. As I looked towards the shrub where the unusual trousers had been discarded, I made an inexplicable decision in retrospect: I decided to retrieve those trousers. I needed to act that very night, as there was always a gatekeeper near the bush during the day. Additionally, there was a possibility that we might be transferred to another camp the next day, which would eliminate any opportunity to reclaim them.

That night had some dim moonlight, I was able to see the bush not too far away. Because my foot was hurt and I couldn't walk, I started to crawl slowly toward the bush. Late at night, it was so quiet, not even a single sound. I just kept crawling slowly. When crawling near the tents, I suddenly heard someone snoring. Looking in that direction, I was horrified to discover that three or four Pol Pot soldiers were sleeping there. Their guns were hung on bamboo poles near where they slept. My heart was pounding: They had already spared my life once this afternoon. At that time, if I were caught by them again, I would surely be executed!

I was so scared. I wanted to turn back, but anyway, I had already crawled more than half the distance. And I thought to myself that without gold, how would I be able to survive in the coming days, how would I be able to return the gold that I borrowed from my cousin... Well, I was at the point of no return. I had to take a risk. I kept crawling, and my heart was pounding, hoping that Buddha would bless me.

A few minutes later, when I reached the bush, I began to search for my pants. Thank God, my hand touched those "weird" pants!

I started to crawl back to my place. Late at night, there was still no sound. Even the sounds of insects were absent. Only the small snoring sounds of the Pol Pot soldiers. The moonlight helped me crawl back to my tree. Then I quickly hid the pants in a nearby bush and fell asleep until morning.

*

After lunch, still rice with salt, Pol Pot soldiers began to take the afternoon nap. I secretly took out the pants from the bush next to me. Several people in the group were surprised to see those pants. I told them all the details of what I did late last night. Everyone thought I was too reckless. I planned to take out the gold and then get rid of those pants. Looking around, I grabbed a small piece of scrap metal and used it to cut the thread on the hem of my pants to get the gold out.

A Cambodian child, approximately four years of age, stood nearby, observing us with a curious gaze. He may have never encountered Vietnamese individuals before. I proceeded to cut the sewn thread on the hem of the first pant leg and gradually retrieved the gold. Placing the gold on a small rock in front of me, I then began to cut the hem thread on the second pant leg. At this point, I noticed that the child had disappeared...

The gold pieces from the second trouser leg were about to be taken out, and then I suddenly heard the yell of several Pol Pot soldiers running toward me. My brother saw that. He quickly grabbed the pants that I was taking out of the gold and tried to hide them in the bushes nearby, but it was too late because the Pol Pot soldiers had already arrived. A Pol Pot soldier discovered that these soldiers' pants were the ones they had thrown into the bushes yesterday. He got angry and fiercely kicked my brother, causing him to fall to the ground. They took all the gold and the pants and left. The other people in the group and I could only look at my brother with pity but couldn't do anything because we were too scared. It turned out that the four-year-old boy ran back to the tent to tell his father about the gold.

My brother and I lost all the gold and were beaten. We were completely broke! All the gold our parents gave us to escape had now been robbed. My brother slowly crawled to the tree nearby and lay there. He must be in pain! I looked at my brother with pity and tears. Too depressed by the situation, I put my head down on the tree next to me and fell asleep without even realizing it. Dinner that day was the same as usual: rice and salt.

Chapter 5

Reaching the Boundless Sky of Freedom

At night, I struggled to sleep. My mind was preoccupied with concerns for the forthcoming days and the current situation of our family in Vietnam. If the authorities discovered that my brother and I had escaped, would they investigate our household and trouble my parents? I pondered whether my brother regretted fleeing with me and if the other three were experiencing similar distress. After four days without medical attention, my foot had become severely swollen, and its condition was worsening, raising my concern about the potential loss of mobility. Observing around me, it was evident that everyone else was sound asleep, while I alone remained restless throughout the night. Undoubtedly, my circumstances appeared particularly dire.

The next morning, two Pol Pot soldiers came and told everyone to line up. The Tra Vinh Khmer friend interpreted that we were preparing to move to the concentration camp. We started to walk again: one Pol Pot soldier took the lead and then the six of us, then another Pol Pot soldier was in the rear. This trip was different from the previous trip three days ago because the Tra Vinh Khmer friend was able to translate. The two sides easily communicated and understood each other.

Due to my injured foot, I consistently remained at the back of the group. My brother continued to assist me with walking despite his feet being significantly swollen. The trail was dry as it had not rained for several days, and the forest became increasingly sparse as we proceeded. We were informed that the concentration camp was situated at the forest's edge, leading me to conclude that our arrival was imminent.

The pain in my foot continued to afflict me, making it difficult to walk. Without my brother's assistance, I would have been unable to proceed. We moved forward quietly, resembling a group of prisoners of war being escorted. No one had the energy to converse, but we all silently hoped to reach Thailand as soon as possible. After several days without the opportunity to bathe, we were not only uncomfortable but also unpleasantly odorous. The dry-mud stains on my shirt, mixed with the sweat from my body, make me smell horrible! Despite my swollen left foot, I continued to press forward. Experiencing dizziness and shortness of breath, I endured significant discomfort throughout this arduous journey to freedom. Had I been aware of the extent of this hardship, I might have reconsidered embarking on it. Nonetheless, surrendering is not an option at this stage. I must persist with the circumstances as they are. I reminded myself that a bit more effort could potentially lead me to reach the concentration camp. This thought motivated me to keep moving forward…

*

That afternoon, we finally arrived at the concentration camp. The two Pol Pot soldiers handed us over to another group of Pol Pot soldiers, and then they returned. This place was still under the control of Pol Pot's remnants. Upon arrival, we joined a group of several dozen individuals who had also escaped. The six of us were provided with essential supplies, including a bag of rice, a bottle of cooking oil, and a lighter. We discovered an abandoned plastic cup and an empty iron barrel that had previously contained cooking oil, likely left by earlier arrivals. We then repurposed the iron barrel as a cooking pot.

Initially, our primary task was to prepare lunch. Everyone was designated a unique responsibility. The location was situated at the forest's edge, adjacent to a small pond. We also utilized an iron barrel to cook rice. Post-meal, we repurposed the same barrel to boil pond water for drinking purposes. In the afternoon, the barrel was further employed to fetch water for bathing and laundry.

The six of us currently had only one set of clothes each. As a man, bathing and washing clothes was relatively straightforward. However, I couldn't help but empathize with the women still detained in this camp, as their situation was undoubtedly more challenging.

There were many groups like ours in the camp. Each group was responsible for its well-being. The only exception was cooking, as everyone relied on the water source from the pond adjacent to the camp. Upon inquiry, I discovered that the longest-staying group had been present for at least ten days, with new arrivals each day. When enough individuals had assembled, the International Red Cross would send a delegation to accompany us. Observing the camp, it was evident that it was already quite crowded. I estimated that the delegation's arrival to rescue us would be imminent.

Our team collected tree branches to construct a simple shelter for overnight accommodation. Unfortunately, although the rain was not torrential that night, it was sufficient to leave us drenched. The cold was such that we had to huddle together to maintain warmth and remain alert until morning.

The following day, at sunrise, I ventured outside to enjoy the warmth of the sun. My brother remained inside the hut with several other individuals. The two Cho Lon Chinese rarely interacted with us due to their limited proficiency in Vietnamese. My cousin sat nearby under a tree, with no one engaging in conversation. Each person seemed lost in their thoughts.

I was particularly concerned about my injured foot, which had sustained damage on the first day we entered the forest. It had been exactly five days without treatment, resulting in significant swelling and persistent pain. I suspected there was considerable pus accumulation. I feared that without prompt medical attention, my foot might deteriorate severely.

I hoped for an influx of new arrivals at the camp soon so we could meet the required quota, prompting an earlier visit from the Red Cross.

At noon, another group of people also was brought to the camp by Pol Pot soldiers. I was so happy I tried to crawl over to observe the situation: A group of seven or eight people, including two girls, had just arrived. The two girls appeared tired and weak. I also experienced injuries... Yesterday, individuals in the camp shared stories about girls who had escaped by land. I reflected on how much longer such circumstances would continue for Vietnamese people.

That night was calm, with no rain. I looked up at the stars in the sky and hoped we would be taken to the Red Cross refugee camp soon. I continued thinking until I was very tired. Then, I fell asleep without realizing it.

*

The following morning, upon waking, I observed numerous Pol Pot soldiers moving around the camp, engaged in cleaning activities. Occasionally, the Pol Pot leader would address a select few individuals. After inquiring with several people, I surmised that the Red Cross might be arriving today to facilitate our departure. Eventually, this news spread throughout the entire camp, resulting in an outburst of joy among all the occupants.

At approximately 10 am, a cloud of road dust became visible in the distance. Due to the considerable distance, specific details about the dust cloud remained unclear. The entire camp was filled with excitement and anticipation, speculating that the International Red Cross delegation had arrived with trucks to transport us. Suggestions were made to determine who among us had the keenest eyesight to climb a tree and identify the source of the dust. A perceptive child volunteered for the task, ascending a tree to observe the distant scene. Upon returning, he reported seeing several trucks bearing Red Cross flags. This news prompted widespread celebration within the camp, as it signified our impending rescue!

Approximately thirty minutes later, loud voices were heard emanating from the bushes surrounding the camp. A group of individuals emerged, holding radios and speaking loudly. Several Caucasian individuals appeared before my eyes. Accompanying them were people dressed in military uniforms that did not resemble those of Pol Pot's soldiers. The camp residents speculated that they might be Thai soldiers. They proceeded to engage in conversation with the leader of Pol Pot's forces.

Approximately 15 minutes later, we were instructed to assemble and follow the group comprising Caucasian individuals and Thai soldiers to the trucks stationed nearby. Observing the Red Cross flag and the Thailand flag on these vehicles brought us immense relief. Some individuals were overcome with emotion and began to cry. Subsequently, we were systematically escorted onto the trucks to be transported to the refugee camp.

It was heartening to see the Red Cross and Thailand flags. The profound emotions experienced by those who had escaped and just reached freedom were beyond description. The sky of freedom lay open before us. My brother, overwhelmed with emotion, said with a trembling voice, "*Brother Fifth, we have arrived in Thailand.*" I embraced him as tears streamed down my face.

I extend my gratitude to Brother Sixth for aiding in my escape. Without his assistance, I would likely have perished in the forest. I am also thankful to my friends in the group for their efforts in saving my life during such trying times. I appreciate Tra Vinh Khmer friend, for rescuing me when I was at risk due to my unusual attire. My thanks go out to the Cambodian traders who guided me and provided me with water. The cost we paid for our freedom was unimaginable. However, I was elated to have reached freedom while the Sisophon forest, known as the forest of death, receded into the distance...

*

The Red Cross delegation transported us by truck to a location near the edge of the forest. The area was uninhabited. Ahead of us was a trench approximately ten meters wide and three meters deep, extending beyond the visible horizon. This trench marked the boundary between Thailand and Cambodia and was later identified as a defensive measure to prevent Vietnamese soldiers from entering Thai territory. Our camp was situated to the east of this trench, remaining within Cambodian territory. The refugee camp was designated as NW9, which stands for Northwest 9. The origin of this name remains unknown to me.

We were escorted across the bridge to enter the camp. Numerous individuals within the camp noticed our arrival and hurried out, hoping to find newly arrived relatives. Suddenly, I heard my cousin exclaim, "*Brother Bac! Brother Bac!*"

Bac reunited with his younger brother, Quan, whom he believed to have been lost. Both brothers expressed their relief through tears, having previously thought the other had perished. Bac was fortunate to reach Thailand without being captured by Pol Pot soldiers.

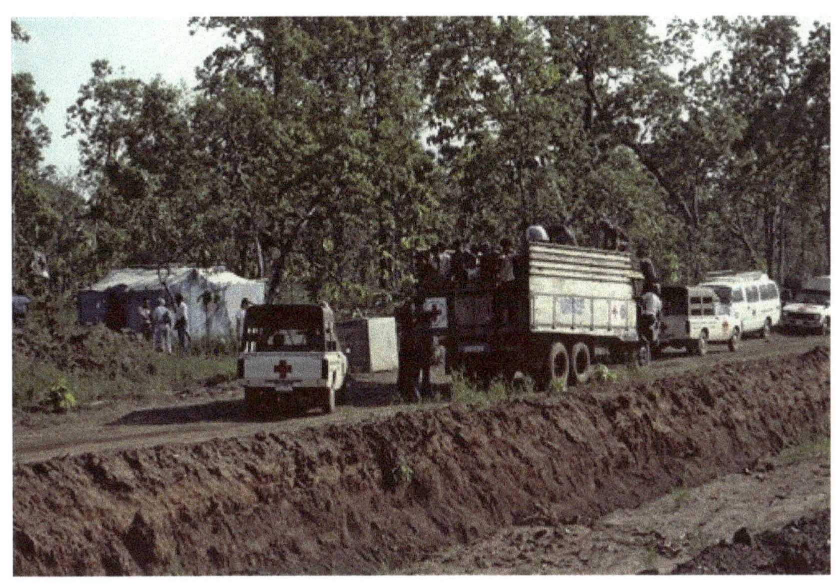

Photo of International Red Cross trucks transporting refugees, parked at the trench near camp NW9, by Yannick Muller, 1980.

The camp staff provided us with the necessary supplies and then assigned us to a tent within the camp. Four of us shared a tent with two additional individuals. Some members of our group began transporting bamboo trees to construct makeshift beds. Meanwhile, I was promptly taken to the medical station. This facility consisted of a simple room managed by a doctor and a nurse, both of whom were Vietnamese refugees. The doctor informed me that had my arrival been delayed any further, there would have been a risk of gangrene necessitating amputation. After thoroughly cleaning and disinfecting the wound, he advised me to return every few days for bandage changes by the nurse.

From that point onward, I navigated the camp with a noticeable limp, whether obtaining food and water, visiting the administration room to read the news, or interacting with new groups of refugees entering the camp. Due to the severity of my injury and malnutrition, my recovery required several months. Consequently, the camp residents referred to me as "Fifth Limp," acknowledging me as the fifth child who walked with a limp!

*

Conditions in the camp were deteriorating as the number of arrivals increased daily. The Red Cross appeared to lack the resources to care for the growing population adequately: The daily rice supplies, purchased directly from local Thai farmers, were consistently insufficient. The Red Cross made efforts to coordinate with the central office and Thai authorities to establish a supply chain for rice and other foodstuffs from larger cities. Meanwhile, refugees in camp NW9 subsisted on whatever food could be sourced locally.

Several weeks after arriving at the camp, everyone was provided with an allocation of four liters of water per day and one bowl of cooked rice to be distributed among six people. Upon receiving the cooked rice, we placed the bowl on the floor to distribute it equally into six cups. The eldest member of our group used a spoon to allocate portions of rice into each person's cup, continuing this process until the entire bowl was emptied. The camp leader urged us to endure these challenging conditions until additional rice supplies from the central government began to arrive.

The scarcity of food, water, medicine, and proper hygiene poses significant threats to our well-being. Prolonged exposure to these conditions may lead to fatalities due to starvation or disease. During mealtimes, there were many flies present, requiring us to wave our hands to keep them away frequently.

During our youth, my brother and I faced significant challenges as young men. With only one small cup of cooked rice per day, sustaining ourselves over a prolonged period seemed impossible. We became exceptionally thin, reminiscent of malnourished prisoners of war. We had no choice but to endure these hardships with resilience.

Many nights, I dreamed of being back with my family in Saigon. Although not wealthy, my parents ensured we had three meals a day. This separation marked our first departure from our family, and I feared it would be a permanent farewell. The prospect of never seeing our parents again was daunting. Upon waking from such dreams, I often felt deep frustration with our present circumstances, longing for an escape from this distressing reality; I wished I wouldn't wake up anymore!

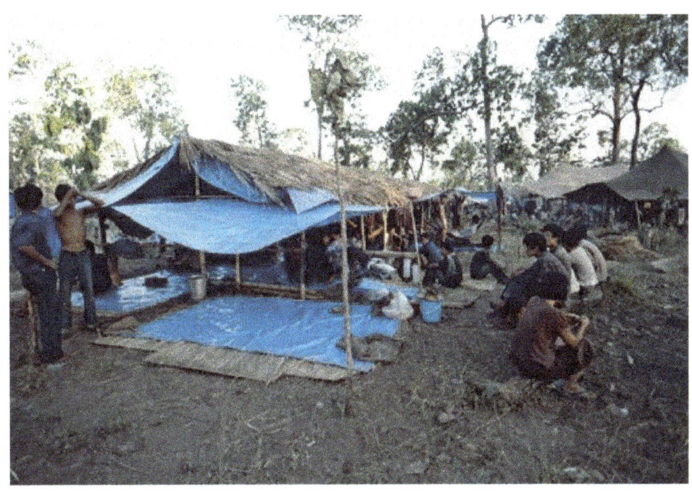

Picture of a refugee tent in camp NW9 by Yannick Muller photographed in 1980

Subsequently, the Thai government officially granted asylum to individuals who had escaped by land. Consequently, I observed numerous aid vehicles arriving at the camp in turns. Our nutritional status improved rapidly: rice was abundant, and meals now included soup. Each person received 15 liters of water per day. The sanitation facilities in the camp also saw significant improvements, and the wound on my foot gradually healed. At night, the camp remained without lights or electricity. When there was moonlight, we would gather and converse until late hours. On nights without moonlight, we retired early when darkness fell. Thus, we spent our days...

During my time in camp NW9, I was pleased to reconnect with several childhood friends from our former neighborhood in Go Dau. However, this happiness was short-lived as my friends conveyed the unfortunate news that a distant relative of mine, along with one of our childhood peers, who had both attempted to escape by land two months prior to my arrival, had not reached their intended destination of freedom. There has been no information regarding their whereabouts for several months, leading to the distressing possibility that they may have perished.

Upon our arrival at the camp, the Red Cross provided us with an envelope bearing a Red Cross stamp to use for writing a letter to inform our families of our safe arrival at the refugee camp. However, several months had elapsed, and I had yet to receive a response. Life in this NW9 camp was quite bleak; we primarily ate and waited for our transfer to a camp further within Thai territory. The camp, surrounded by forests, was still situated within Cambodian territory. Despite the presence of Thai soldiers as camp guards and regular visits from Red Cross officers, we lived in constant fear of potential attacks by Pol Pot soldiers or Vietnamese soldiers.

*

One day, near dinner time, we heard gunshots and artillery shells in the distance. It appeared that there was a conflict involving the Thai army and Vietnamese soldiers somewhere in the area... The gunfire was approaching the camp. Suddenly, there was a loud explosion. People evacuated the camp and moved through the trenches into Thai territory. But the trenches were too deep; jumping down was difficult, and climbing up was even harder. Thousands of individuals in the camp panicked and began to rush across it, creating an extremely chaotic scene. The cries of children who had been separated from their parents mingled with the screams of elderly men and women who were unable to climb over obstacles. My situation was even more dire due to my injured foot, leaving me immobilized. As I stood helplessly in the trench, fearing an attack by Vietnamese soldiers, I suddenly heard a voice calling: *"Brother Fifth, give me your hand."* Looking towards the direction of the voice, I identified the person as my brother.

He had managed to climb to the opposite side of the trench and, aware of my inability to climb over, ran along the trench searching for me despite the nearby gunfire. Eventually, he located me and pulled me up. We then made our way towards Thai territory to evade danger. However, shortly after, Thai soldiers apprehended us.

Luckily, the gunfire became less and less frequent and stopped altogether. Perhaps the Vietnamese soldiers gave up and retreated. Then, the Thai army chased all the refugees back to the camp that night. Too shocked by the incident and afraid that it could happen again any time, I couldn't sleep all night.

The duration spent in the NW9 camp felt extensive and monotonous. At times, when homesickness or sorrow about my current situation overwhelmed me, I would sing the song "NW9," composed by musician Minh Duy, within the camp. This song encapsulated the emotions of Vietnamese refugees residing in the NW9 camp, including sadness, deprivation, fear, and loneliness, as they anxiously awaited their future day by day. I transcribed the lyrics of the song and have preserved them for over 45 years. Whenever I have to perform it again, it elicits the same profound sense of unease within me...

*

One day, I reviewed the transfer list for the first time. Individuals with young children or those who are elderly were given priority. I was very pleased to see the list, as this indicates that our turn will come in due course.

One morning, as per my usual routine over the past few months, I proceeded to the office to review the transfer list. I was pleased to find our names prominently displayed on the list. Filled with joy, I promptly returned to inform my brother and cousins of the news. They were all very pleased to learn that our transfer date was approaching.

A few days later, the four of us were transferred to Phanat Nikhom camp in Chonburi province, where we were interviewed by the U.S. delegation and subsequently approved for settlement in the United States.

In February 1981, we arrived in the United States, fulfilling our dream of settling in America. I am grateful for God's protection that enabled our safe arrival despite numerous hardships and dangers. Our sincere appreciation goes to the United States for welcoming Vietnamese refugees, as well as other refugees. We extend our gratitude to the International Red Cross for their dedicated teams stationed deep in the jungle to assist us. Our thanks also go to the Thai government for establishing refugee camps providing temporary residence while awaiting settlement in a third country. Finally, I am deeply thankful for my parents' sacrifice; allowing two children to escape was an immense emotional, life-threatening, and financial risk. Now that I am married with children, I have a greater understanding of my parents' boundless love.

Eventually, the aspiration of attending university for a man who was often frail and unwell during his youth was realized. I completed my studies with an engineering degree and dedicated exactly 35 years to my profession before retiring. Numerous times, I contemplated rewriting my memoir recounting our escape, only to abandon the notion an equal number of times. Perhaps life's demands diverted my focus. Nonetheless, the memories have remained vivid. Now, I am compelled to document the events of our arduous and perilous journey in pursuit of freedom. The cost of this liberty was paid with our lives. I hope that my children and grandchildren will comprehend the sacrifices their ancestors made to secure this valuable freedom.

*

Forty-five years have elapsed, and I once believed that escape stories were a thing of the past. However, such occurrences continue in various countries around the globe. Even in Vietnam, my birthplace, although life has improved a lot, there are still people who want to leave the country!

I pray for a peaceful world where people no longer must flee their homes due to political oppression so that they don't have to endure great hardship and danger like I went through…

California, 2025

Autumn Wind

In the autumn of 2024, during a walk by the lake near my residence, I noticed the leaves falling and being carried away by the wind. One afternoon, the moonlight was especially gentle. This scene brought back memories of an evening 45 years ago when, under similar moonlit skies, I experienced significant fear while fleeing my homeland. Inspired by the scenery, I wrote the poem "Autumn Wind" to express my long-held feelings after living in a new country, distant from my homeland. It is my aspiration that this poem effectively communicates some of my most profound emotions to the readers.

The autumn wind ripples the lake's surface
Like time flies - waiting for no one
Autumn leaves flow with the wind
My life had passed through difficult days…
Remember the old days playing with children in the village
Shooting marbles, fighting crickets without caring about the future…
When I think back now - so emotional:
My homeland is far away, will I return tomorrow?
Looking at the falling leaves - so sad
They flow with the wind - Like me, no better
Floating with fate – Can't resist it…
Remember the days I left for the faraway land
Overwhelm with dangers with a worrisome mind
With old memories, I love my parents so much
They sacrificed everything – but only got troubles
Hope for their children would soon flourish
Blossom in the foreign land and glory to the homeland
And now life has blossomed
Thanks to the new land that erased old sorrows
*

Feeling the cold wind on my shoulders
Why do I keep remembering the past?

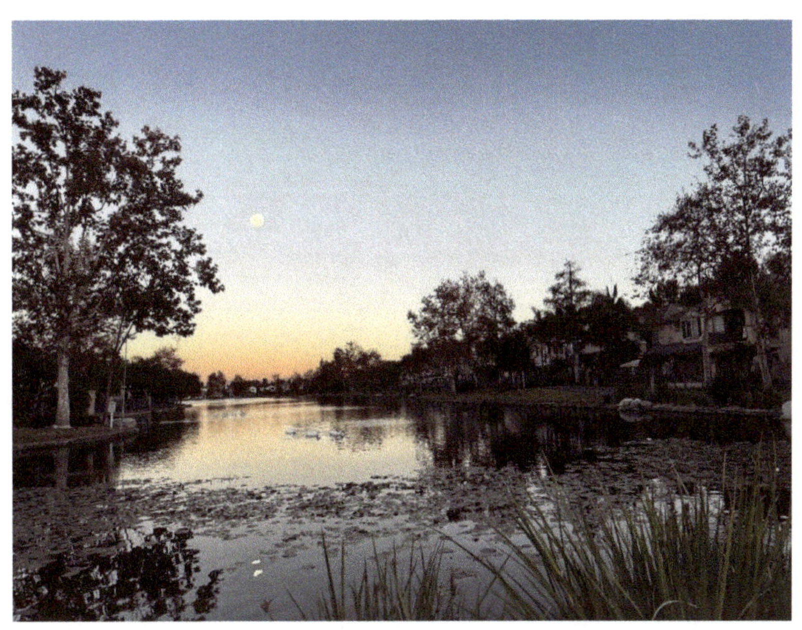

This photograph captures the lake situated in the park adjacent to my family's residence. I make it a routine to walk around the lake twice daily, in the early morning and late afternoon, completing a minimum of two laps each time. The picturesque view of leaves cascading and being carried away by the breeze, along with the enchanting moonlight, evokes a deep emotional response within me, inspiring the creation of my poem titled "Autumn Wind."

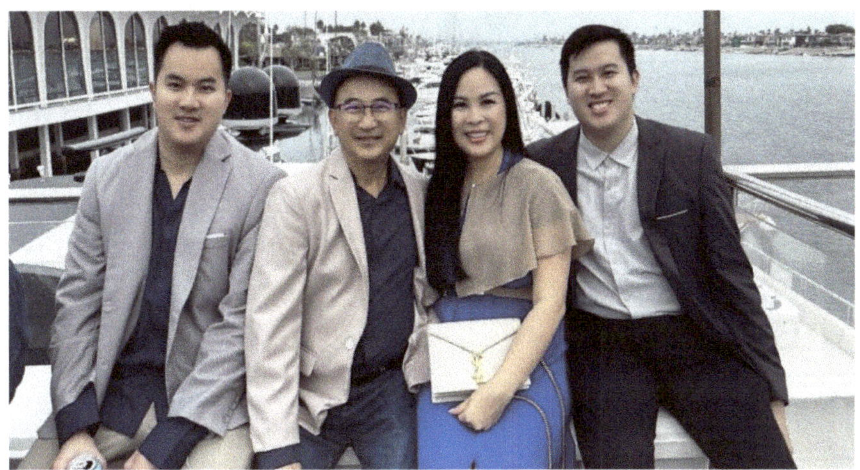

Photo of the author's family, October 2024, Newport Beach, California (Left to right: older son, author, wife, younger son)

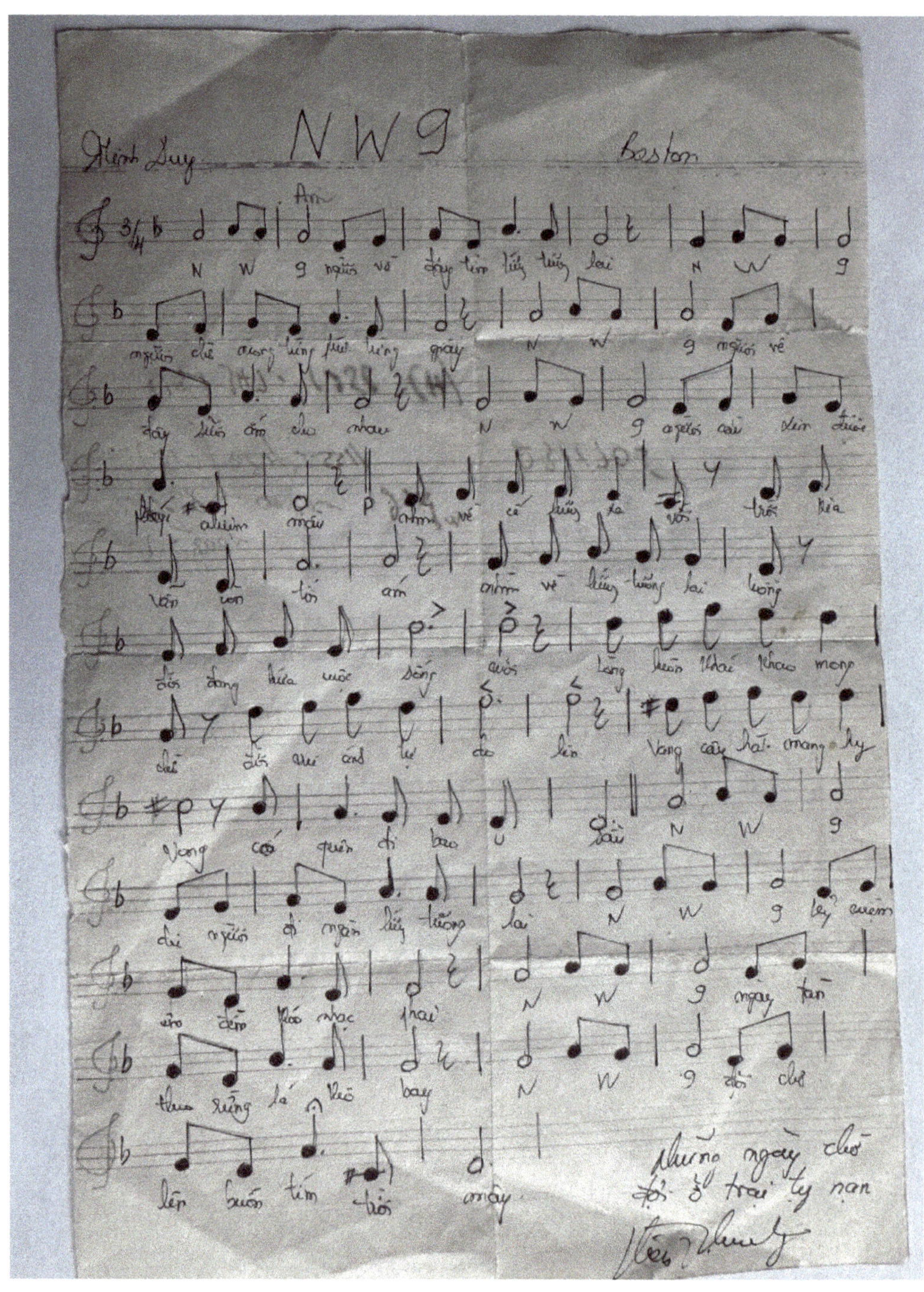

The song NW9 was transcribed manually by the author while residing in camp NW9 in 1980.

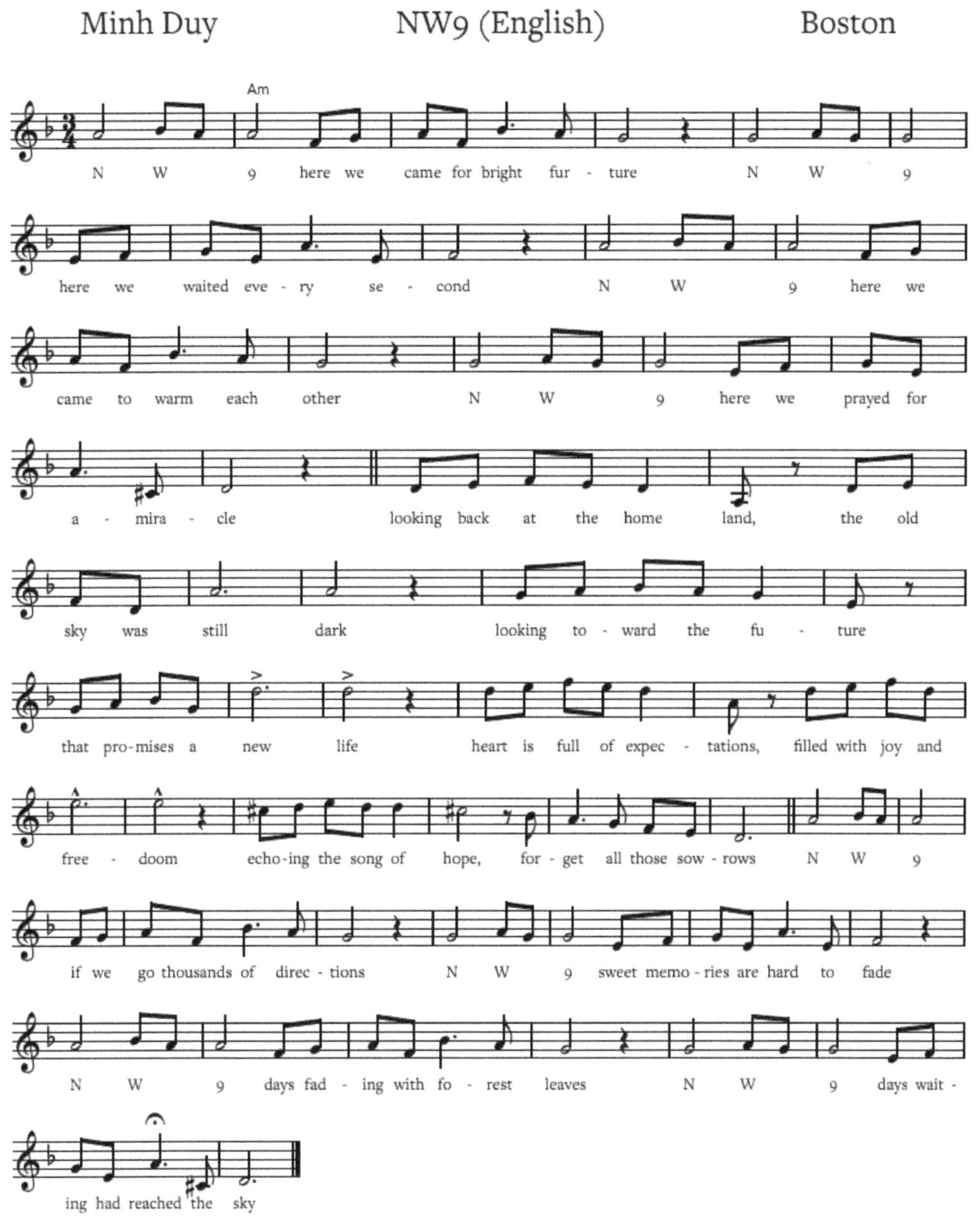

Thanks to the musician Minh Duy for composing this song. It is intended to be preserved and shared with future generations.